We Get Up!

Illustr

MW01009125

Target Skill Review

Scott Foresman
is an imprint of

PEARSON

The sun sets.

Rex gets in bed.

Fred gets up.

He will get the milk to us.

Lil jumps up.

She will get the buns for us.

Bill gets up.

He will get the newspaper to us.

Dot gets up.

She will get Mom to us.

Matt gets up.

He will get his hat and rig.

Rex and the sun get up.

Fred, Lil, Bill, and Dot get in bed.